Australian Biographical Monographs

4

Australian Biographical Monographs

Series Editor: Scott Prasser

Previous Volumes

1
Joseph Lyons and the Management of Adversity
Kevin Andrews

2
Harold Holt and the Liberal Imagination
Tom Frame

3
Johannes Bjelke-Petersen
Bruce Kingston

Australian Biographical Monographs
4

Lindsay Thompson
Character, Competence and Conviction

William Westerman

Connor Court Publishing

Published in 2020 by Connor Court Publishing Pty Ltd

Connor Court Publishing Pty Ltd
PO Box 7257
Redland Bay QLD 4165
sales@connorcourt.com
www.connorcourt.com
Phone 0497-900-685

Printed in Australia

ISBN: 9781922449139

Front cover design: Maria Giordano

Front cover image courtesy of the Thompson family

This book is dedicated to
Francis James Lesock (1923-2015)

Australian Biographical Monographs

Series overview

The Connor Court Publishing's Australian Biographical Series on past leading Australian political leaders and other important figures seeks to provide an overview for those who are unfamiliar with the subject and to highlight the person's particular importance, controversies and contributions to Australia's progress.

The monographs are scholarly rather than academic in focus placing emphasis on a clear narrative, but with careful attention to referencing to ensure views expressed are supported by appropriate sources and evidence.

The Series was initiated because of the decline in the study of Australian history at our schools and universities and the consequential lack of knowledge or even worse, distorted views of some of Australia's leading figures who deserve to be remembered, understood for both their achievements, and as each volume also highlights, their flaws.

This monograph by historian Dr William Westerman on Premier Lindsay Thompson, one of the longest serving members and successful ministers in Victorian Liberal administrations from 1955-1982 was overdue. Too few appreciate his achievements. Highly competent and unusual in politics, highly respected by all sides of politics, this biography traces his rise from backbencher to minister where in the key portfolios of education and housing he made many initiatives. More importantly, this monograph highlights Lindsay Thompson's very style and approach to politics. It was one based on clear principles, focussing on the problem at hand and seeking long term solutions. No scandal erupted around his term in office. His legacy is great and hopefully this thoroughly researched monograph will bring to the attention of others, especially those in the Victorian Liberal Party, what being a Liberal is all about.

- Dr Scott Prasser, May 2020

'A successful member of parliament must have four qualities: he must know his stuff, he must not be conceited, he must be a decent chap, finally he must be respected by both sides as a man.'

Clement Attlee,
Prime Minister of the United Kingdom (1945-1951)

Introduction

On the evening of 4 November 1982, members of the Victorian Legislative Assembly returned to the chamber following a recess for dinner. Premier John Cain junior, triumphant from the Australian Labor Party's (ALP) first electoral victory in Victoria since the 1950s, now stood at the despatch box on the treasury benches. Addressing the Speaker, he asked for leave to bring forward the following motion:

> That this House places on record its appreciation of the distinguished services rendered to the Parliament and the people of Victoria by the Honourable Lindsay Hamilton Simpson Thompson, C.M.G., M.P., as member of the Legislative Council for the electoral province of Higinbotham from 1955 to 1967 and for the electoral province of Monash from 1967 to 1970, as member of the Legislative Assembly for the electoral district of Malvern from 1970 to 1982 and as Premier from 5 June 1981 to 8 April 1982, in addition to his other important offices as Minister of the Crown and as Leader of the Opposition, during the period 1958 to 1982.[1]

Thompson, Cain's vanquished opponent, was sitting on the opposition benches for the first time since 1955. He had just announced his retirement from politics, and was possibly hoping to slip away from Spring Street quietly.[2] Cain did not give him that opportunity. He knew how highly the members of parliament respected Thompson, and he wanted to give them the chance to express their gratitude for his contribution to public life.[3] Accordingly, 21 members of the Legislative Assembly – nine Liberal, two National and ten Labor – rose to speak to the motion.

It was an unconventional moment. Ordinarily, condolence motions were the only reason members of different parties would offer a tribute to a former parliamentarian. While there was little political risk for the newly-elected government to honour Thompson in this manner, there was also no reason to do so unless the sentiments were genuine. One opposition member noted that he had 'heaped a fair bit of abuse on [Thompson's] head' in the past, but declared that 'if each or any one of us can retire with as much honour as Lindsay, then we will have done damned well'.[4] How did Lindsay Thompson, a long-serving minister who held several controversial portfolios, manage to retire from politics with such esteem? In answering that question, this book will explore the political career of a remarkable yet almost entirely overlooked figure in twentieth-century Victorian politics.

Premier for only ten months, Thompson served as the night-watchman for a government in decline. He had little time to leave a legacy as Premier, and is overshadowed by the man he replaced, Dick Hamer, and the man who defeated him, John Cain junior. Yet he served in Cabinet for over two decades, including nine years as Hamer's deputy. His most prominent role was Minister for Education, which he held for a record 12 years. It was a staggering length of time in such a demanding and controversial portfolio. As the new Labor Minister for Education, Robert Fordham, remarked, 'as one who had held that portfolio for six months ... I have no wish to emulate the record of my distinguished predecessor.'[5] He also spent six years as Minister for Housing (itself an overlooked aspect of his career). Both portfolios affected the lives of thousands of Victorians, yet they are not normally considered as the crowning achievements of a well-studied figure in Australian political history. The most notable episode during his time in parliament, his role in the Faraday kidnapping in 1972, had almost nothing to do with politics or policy, although it revealed why many regarded him so highly.

While this book does not present a comprehensive account of Lindsay Thompson's life and career, it does argue that he was a remarkable parliamentarian and a man worthy of study. This is not to suggest that he was not without faults, nor that his political views were unimpeachable. He was a classical liberal in the Menzies tradition, and he held views with which others, particularly within the ALP and the trade union movement, ardently disagreed. The fact that he was a conviction politician yet still managed to emerge from the cauldron of politics with such universal regard speaks even more highly of his conduct while he was a member of parliament.

The way his political opponents acknowledged Thompson

upon his retirement offers a stark contrast to the lack of trust and respect in which many current politicians are held. This book explores the development of his character and political conviction, as he learned and refined the art and science of parliamentary process and public administration. While not without flaws and certainly the beneficiary of good fortune, he is nevertheless worthy of examination, recognition and, for contemporary and future elected officials, emulation.

Formative years

It is not a peculiarly imaginative claim to say that Lindsay Thompson was a product of the time and place in which he was raised. This is worth noting, however, as the Australia of the 1920s, 1930s and 1940s was radically different from the cosmopolitan Australia of the twenty-first century. Born on 15 October 1923, he grew up in a country still recovering from the Great War, one that would also endure the hardships of the Great Depression. At the time, Australian citizens were also British subjects. King George V was Australia's monarch and reigned over the sprawling British Empire at its territorial peak. The White Australia policy had strong support from all sides of politics, while the authorities had forced many Indigenous Australians onto reserves or missions.

Lindsay's early years were tragically affected by the death of his father, Arthur, when he was three years old. His mother, Ethel, had worked as a teacher and would have struggled to raise Lindsay had it not been for the support of her mother. Sarah Simpson had been among the first group of female teachers employed by the Victorian Education Department in 1872 and, since her retirement in 1894, had received a generous pension. In addition to supporting the household financially, she taught Lindsay 'the rudiments of reading, writing and arithmetic' for the first nine years of his life.[6] The family lived in Glen Iris until 1928, when, to make life easier, they moved in with Ethel's older sister, Effie, and her family in Elsternwick. Like Ethel, Effie was also a teacher. In fact, in

1889 the four Simpson sisters had established what became Mentone Girls' Grammar School, with Effie as the school's first headmistress. Thus from a young age, education was a large part of Lindsay's life.

By no means the beneficiary of an affluent upbringing, he and his family were nevertheless set apart from the working class, those who relied on manual labour for income. As a result, Lindsay was imbued with many of the cultural, social and political assumptions and values usually held by middle-class Australians of that era. Rather than defining themselves by a collective identity, historian Judith Brett argued that such Australians saw themselves as individuals whose sense of identity derived from their individual attributes and moral qualities.[7] Lindsay would certainly develop respect for such thinking. In 1969, when discussing state education, he argued that education's most important aim was 'to develop a healthy set of values in younger people', reinforcing high moral standards, and fostering integrity, tolerance, unselfishness, a capacity for service and respect for law and order.[8] Being raised in the Protestant tradition further reinforced particular moral and philosophical views; Protestantism affirmed a commitment to the morally independent individual, over and against the rigid tribalism of Roman Catholicism.[9]

Schooling proved an influential period of Lindsay's early life, providing opportunities for both structured education and extra-curricular activities. In 1929 he began attending Caulfield Grammar School in East St Kilda. Sarah Simpson had been providing for the family from her pension, and when she died in 1933, money was allocated from her estate to allow Lindsay to continue his private schooling. When his family funds disappeared in 1936 after the bankruptcy of the family's solicitor, the headmaster retained Lindsay as a pupil on a scholarship, for which he was deeply grateful. The scholarship required him to maintain a high academic standard. In retrospect, he viewed this as an advantage rather than a liability as it helped him develop an impressive work ethic and drove him to be Dux of the School in his final year.[10]

At Caulfield, many of Lindsay Thompson's defining aspects, particularly his leadership ability, debating prowess and penchant for sport, were evident. In 1941, his final year, not only was he Captain of the School and Captain of the House, he captained both the First XI cricket team and the school debating team.[11] Sport, in particular, held such a high place in his life that it became a lens through which he interpreted and communicated. It also reinforced certain virtues, such as teamwork and fair play, that he would carry with him for the rest of his life.

Leaving school, he sought employment where he could (including teaching at his former school) until April 1942, when he enlisted in the Second Australian Imperial Force. Allotted to the Australian Corps of Signals, in September 1943 he deployed to New Guinea as part of Headquarters

New Guinea Force in Port Moresby. Twelve months later he moved across the Owen Stanley Ranges to Headquarters First Australian Army when it arrived in Lae. Primarily confined to headquarters, his war service in New Guinea was unremarkable, with two exceptions. First, he developed several medical conditions, particularly malaria, that afflicted him throughout the remainder of his life. Second, he gained a valuable sense of perspective. Many of his friends from school enlisted in the Services; 'they did not come back', Thompson noted in 1982, 'I did'.[12]

Discharged from the army in late October 1945, he availed himself of the Commonwealth Reconstruction Training Scheme and enrolled at the University of Melbourne in 1946. Having studied Latin by correspondence while in New Guinea, he now read history and political science as part of a Bachelor of Arts.[13] Continuing higher education allowed him to develop his political thought, his skills in written and oral communication and debate, as well as indulge his various sporting passions. University contemporaries noted his near-obsession with football (particularly the Richmond Football Club), football statistics and a large blue RAAF greatcoat that he wore year in, year out.[14] Following his Honours year, he undertook a Bachelor of Education, after which he held teaching positions at Spring Road Central School, Malvern, and then Melbourne High School.[15]

During his years at university, he met his future wife, Joan Poynder, and in 1948 they announced their engagement.

Married in January 1950, they would have three children together that decade. Although he was making a good life for himself as a teacher, he was soon drawn towards a different vocation. When looking back on the experience of the Second World War, he speculated that many servicemen, and those on the home front, were thinking about the time after the war and were asking themselves 'how can we really build a better world?'[16] Post-war Australian politics actively debated this question, and two competing philosophical ideas vied with each other to provide an answer.

The ALP offered one alternative. In 1949, Labor Prime Minister Ben Chifley famously declared that the labour movement's great objective, 'the light on the hill', was to work for the betterment of humanity, bringing 'something better to the people, better standards of living, greater happiness to the mass of people'.[17] Few from any political persuasion would likely find fault with the aspiration, but as a democratic socialist political party (as stipulated in its constitution) born from the working class and the labour movement, it viewed the country as being divided by class and economic interests. As a consequence, the party often looked to collective and centralised means, such as a more expansive approach to the welfare state or greater state control of the economy, to combat the adverse effects of class division and economic disparity and thus achieve its great objective.

For as long as there had been an ALP, there had been those politically opposed to it for a variety of reasons. In 1944,

Robert Menzies formed the Liberal Party of Australia to draw together the sometimes disparate assortment of centre-right political parties historically in opposition to Labor. Rejecting the labour movement's class or economic-based division of society, the party emphasised the primacy of the individual, advocating the freedom of citizens to choose their own way of living subject to the rights of others. It encouraged individual initiative and enterprise and upheld basic freedoms such as speech, religion and association (foundational personal freedoms, Thompson later wrote, that were 'always dear to me').[18] The party also affirmed that family life was 'fundamental to the well-being of society', and wanted to see every family live in a comfortable home at a reasonable cost and with adequate community amenities.[19] Thompson supported Menzies' emphasis on home ownership, influenced by his experience living with his extended family, as well as the challenge he and Joan faced when finding somewhere to live as newlyweds.[20]

While not explicitly a religious organisation, the Liberal Party drew much of its political imagination from a Reformed well. The vast majority of Australian liberals of the era were Protestants, and, as Judith Brett noted, 'even when they were not, the virtues on which they based their claims to govern were Protestant virtues': independence, loyalty to Empire and reluctance to pursue group-based sectional claims.[21] The Liberal Party thus resonated with Thompson philosophically, politically, socially and theologically. He was also averse to the requirement imposed upon ALP parliamentarians to be bound by caucus decisions, and was generally opposed to the restrictive effects of socialism on the rights of the individual.

Thompson made his first foray into politics in the years immediately following his return from the war. As a sportsman and keen debater, he was likely drawn to the contest of ideas that politics offered. In 1945, through a personal connection, he became involved in Fred Edmunds' campaign for the Victorian state seat of Hawthorn. During the campaign, he met and impressed Menzies himself (then the federal leader of the opposition).[22] Despite his growing interest in politics, Thompson stayed on the margins until 1953, when he began to contest pre-selection ballots for the state Liberal Party, none of which met with success. He described 1954 as 'the worst year of my life'.[23] Not only was he hospitalised by a recurring ailment from his time in New Guinea (which, among other things, required him to re-learn how to walk), but he lost three separate bids for Liberal Party pre-selection.[24]

Then, on 20 November 1954, the sitting member for the Victorian upper house seat of Higinbotham, Sir James Kennedy, died unexpectedly. After his string of pre-selection defeats, Thompson was initially reluctant to contest this new vacancy. Several associates urged him on, however, and he soon defeated 20 other candidates to gain the nomination. Wasting no time, he spent six weeks campaigning for the by-election. Aided by a timely intervention from Menzies,

Thompson was elected to Higinbotham Province on 29 January 1955 with a sizeable majority. He only had a short period in the Legislative Council, however, before he would need to contest the general election later that year.[25] Nevertheless, after a challenging period, he had finally made it to Spring Street. While many of his social and political views were solidly established, they had yet to be tested in a cauldron of public debate, parliamentary process and internal party machinations – all of which lay ahead of him.

Political apprenticeship

Lindsay Thompson arrived in the Victorian Parliament as a handsome, fresh-faced 31-year-old keen to make his mark on state politics. He had barely taken his seat, however, when momentous events reshaped the political landscape in the state and the nation. Indeed, 19 April 1955, his first day sitting in the Legislative Council, was as dramatic as one could hope for in a state parliament. At that time the ALP was in turmoil, coming apart at the seams over the issue of communism, and Premier John Cain senior's government was teetering on the brink of collapse. That evening, fractures in the Labor Party burst forth, with key Labor members in both houses splitting from the party. The opposition leader, Henry Bolte, opportunistically moved a motion of no-confidence, which passed when several dissident Labor members crossed the floor. This act ultimately led to the dissolution of parliament and the demise of the Cain Government.

With a lower house election now scheduled for 28 May, Thompson was quickly put to work drafting education policy for Bolte and his deputy, Arthur Rylah.[26] Following the Liberal Party's resounding victory, he was almost immediately appointed to Cabinet before internal political requirements intervened to thwart what would have been a remarkably rapid rise.[27] Still, he was now a backbencher in the party of government, something that must have seemed improbable only 12 months beforehand. His timing, governed as much by fate as by his actions, could not have been better to set himself up for a long parliamentary career.

On 16 June 1955, he delivered his maiden speech. Laced with British imperial sentiment and showing support for Bolte's legislative agenda, he argued that the 'true wealth of a nation' lay in the character of its people. As such, it was the responsibility of the state to ensure that its education system aided in 'moulding the national character'.[28] A high standard of education was necessary for a democracy to ensure there was an 'enlightened and politically-conscious' population.[29] He also foreshadowed what would become a significant challenge of his later parliamentary career, the increase in school-aged children brought about by the post-war baby boom. Other themes resonated strongly with Menzies' famous 'Forgotten People' speech of 1942, such as the value of the family unit and a 'well-balanced home environment', as well as the importance of housing, particularly for young married couples.[30]

After one year on the backbench, in 1956 he was elected as parliamentary secretary to the Cabinet. This swift advancement allowed him to observe both how Bolte worked as Premier and the nature of his partnership with Rylah (which he would come to admire and emulate). Following the 1958 election, Thompson entered Cabinet when Bolte appointed him Assistant Chief Secretary and Assistant Attorney-General, effectively becoming Rylah's deputy. This period proved invaluable, gaining extensive ministerial experience under Rylah, and being exposed to a wide range of policy and administrative issues. In particular, the Chief Secretary role was an amalgam of responsibilities not contained within any other portfolio, covering, Thompson noted, 'almost everything from Aborigines to the Zoo'.[31]

While it was an intensely busy period, he thrived working at a high tempo. As part of his role in the Legislative Council, he spent considerable time studying legislation and then piloting it through second reading and committee stages. Aware of the calibre of those on the opposition benches, he needed to be thoroughly familiar with each Bill he handled. He developed a habit of studying every clause of a Bill before introducing it and never resorted to using second reading speech notes prepared by the originator department. While this approach added to his preparatory work, it made the actual handling of a Bill 'immeasurably easier'.[32] Throughout his parliamentary career, those on both sides of the chamber would comment on his impressive ability to read details of a second reading speech without drawing on notes.[33]

After three years as Rylah's understudy, following the 1961 election Bolte rewarded him with a promotion to Minister for Housing and Forests, giving him the opportunity to take responsibility for portfolios of his own. Thompson was ready for the formidable and sophisticated task of being a Minister of the Crown, which required him to be an administrator, politician, publicist and advocate, frequently all at once.[34] Forests was relatively relaxed, but Thompson nevertheless threw himself into it with thoroughness and energy. In 1965,

Bolte asked whether he was interested in adding Aboriginal Welfare to his responsibilities. It was a measure of trust and an acknowledgement of the confidence the Premier had in him that he was offered this particular 'political hot potato'.[35] He was indeed interested in that area, and could not help himself from taking up the challenge. Victoria had a much smaller indigenous population than other states, but there were still many acute policy issues to address.[36]

Housing, where he was responsible for overseeing the Housing Commission of Victoria, was perhaps the most difficult of the three portfolios. In addition to the Commission's 'breakneck' tempo of activity, the portfolio was much more controversial and potentially politically damaging than many others in Cabinet.[37] Public housing issues in Melbourne posed complex questions at both a policy and personal level for which there were not necessarily expedient or straightforward answers. Furthermore, newspapers or opposition members were all too willing to bring the human ramifications of policy decisions, such as the eviction of a family, to Thompson's notice in the most public manner.

As Housing Minister, he devoted himself to four areas: slum abolition (a longstanding project for the Housing Commission); the fostering of homeownership; the provision of accommodation for the elderly and the disadvantaged; and developing an accurate estimation of housing demand and need.[38] While each was a pressing concern, inner-city slum abolition and the ensuing construction of public housing became Thompson's most significant legacy as Housing Minister and is illustrative of the manner in which he thought through difficult policy challenges.

Established in 1938, the Housing Commission's aim was to improve existing housing conditions and provide adequate housing for people of limited means (with a strong undercurrent of moralistic social reform).[39] Its initial target was the squalid and impoverished slums in Melbourne's industrial suburbs. The pace and extent of inner-city reclamation ebbed and flowed, and after a period of constructing housing in Melbourne's outer suburbs following the Second World War, it returned to prominence as one of the newly-elected Bolte Government's key policy areas.

Thompson's predecessor, Horace Petty, had re-invigorated the work of slum demolition, but there was still much effort required to construct new public housing on the newly cleared land. When Thompson took over this responsibility, he was faced with the problem of increased project costs: not only were land acquisition and clearance costs increasing, but once the government entered the market to purchase adjacent land for new housing estates, property prices began to soar. Building low-story estates, therefore, became uneconomical. In response, the Commission decided that to make the best use of the limited land available, they would construct high-rise flats instead.[40]

Thompson understood the disadvantages of this course of

action, but supported the decision based upon a reasoned assessment of the situation. The cost of constructing low-rise housing would inhibit the total number constructed, and to build more meant moving to the outer suburbs, further away from the occupants' places of employment. Town planners argued that the number of inner-city residents needed to increase (the total had been dwindling for some time) and that by building in these areas they would make best use of existing water, sewerage and transport services. Furthermore, despite the fact that high-rise towers would be aesthetically incongruous with their surrounding areas, Thompson argued that there was 'no question' they would provide 'far superior and healthier accommodation to the tumble-down shanties and galvanised iron sheds' there previously.[41]

The first multi-storey block erected by the Commission was a 16-storey building in South Melbourne, opened in 1962.[42] Others followed in North Melbourne, Flemington, Fitzroy, Collingwood and Carlton. Despite their pragmatic function, the towers' design and construction was based on the ideas of Swiss modernist architect Le Corbusier, which showed commendable ambition on the part of the Housing Commission. In 1966, the 'Park Towers' block in South Melbourne received international acclaim. Still, many were not enamoured with the new towers; at various times, activist inner-city resident associations, local councils, ethnic groups, conservation organisations and trade unions expressed their opposition. Criticised as 'prisons in the sky', the towers were architecturally dissonant from their surrounding areas and reinforced a division between the 'haves' and the 'have nots'.[43] The passage of time has done little to enhance their reputation.

While the Commission's high-rise towers were far from Thompson's only concern as Housing Minister, they were a particularly prominent accomplishment. For better or worse, they still define part of Melbourne's skyline, standing, in the words of one historian, 'as symbols of a wasting modernist dream'.[44] Decades on, the areas in which they are located are now gentrified, almost beyond recognition from their working-class origins, and the word 'slums' has largely disappeared from the vocabulary of Melburnians. The legacy of the towers remains both heavily contested (one writer described them as being 'as much an impressively cohesive feat of urban planning as they are a problematic symbol of heavy-handed social control') and, due to their looming presence, inescapable.[45]

Thompson's first nine years in Cabinet was both an apprenticeship and a chance to demonstrate his potential for greater things. As Minister for Housing, for instance, he gained experience managing high-profile state government projects with significant ramifications on the life of the city. He thrived under Bolte, who gave his ministers considerable freedom to carry out their responsibilities, provided they remained within their budgets. He developed a reputation as an effective administrator with an impressive command of policy detail who was not afraid to be a hands-on minister. On one occasion he picked 50 names at random from the Housing Commission waiting list and set off with a senior official to call on them at their nominated address. The exercise was 'an eye-opener', and gave him a better appreciation of the application process.[46]

While his decision-making was empirically based, it was always underpinned by broad philosophical assumptions. Promoting homeownership, for instance, was not just about wanting people to enjoy the additional security that owning a home brought, it was also a reflection of his belief that homeowners became more responsible citizens, given that they possessed 'a stake in the kingdom' (to paraphrase a line from Menzies' 'Forgotten People' speech).[47] As demanding as his initial years in Cabinet had been, Bolte soon asked Thompson to apply his experience and abilities to an even more challenging task.

Minister for Education

On 29 April 1967, Victoria returned Henry Bolte and his government for a fifth term. Following the election, Bolte moved the 43-year-old Lindsay Thompson from Housing, Forests and Aboriginal Welfare into his career-defining role. John Bloomfield had been the Minister for Education since 1956. While not yet ready to retire, the 65-year-old believed the time had come to step down from the front bench and hand over the demanding portfolio to a successor. Selected as Bloomfield's replacement, Thompson embarked on 12 years as Minister for Education, eclipsing even his predecessor's extensive tenure.

As important and challenging as his previous portfolios had been, education was a step up from almost all other responsibilities in state Cabinet. The Education Minister controlled the vast state education system (eventually supported by an assistant minister), which aimed to provide every Victorian child, at least until the age of 15, with an education suitable for their age, ability and aptitudes.[48] Indicative of its importance, it accounted for the single most significant slice of the state budget. In 1967, $239.2 million was allocated from the total consolidated revenue fund of $603 million.[49] At that time, the Victorian state school system had 540,281 students at 2,241 schools (the overwhelming majority of which were primary schools).[50] Victoria also had three universities, several institutes of technology, technical and agricultural colleges and the Council of Adult

Education (all of which included an Education Department representative on their councils).[51]

The Director-General of Education ran the department ('a vast, complex and rapidly developing organisation' as Thompson described it), supported by an Assistant Director-General and a clerical division.[52] In 1967, the system employed 24,373 teachers divided into primary, secondary, technical and professional divisions.[53] Their conditions of employment were safeguarded by right of appeal to the Teachers' Tribunal, an independent statutory authority. Several different trade unions also represented teachers' interests, with the Victorian Teachers' Union (VTU) and the Victorian Secondary Teachers' Association (VSTA) the two largest.[54]

Given his background, Thompson came to the portfolio with a well-developed appreciation of the practice and philosophy of education. Mere days after his first election in 1955, he told reporters that education was one of his biggest priorities.[55] His early life allowed him to understand the demands the profession placed upon teachers, and from his personal experience at Caulfield Grammar, he knew what benefits a full education could provide. For him, education was a means for individual advancement as well as social improvement. He believed that schools should foster appropriate values in its students, equipping them both to undertake the challenges of adulthood and for the betterment of society in general. 'In a scientific age', he wrote in 1972, 'there is a danger of overlooking the importance of the teacher's personal qualities.

The latter will always be an important factor in moulding the character of the rising generation.'[56]

He also argued that the education system should aim to let young people fully develop their 'spiritual, mental, physical and creative powers' regardless of their 'colour, class, race or creed', creating 'true equality of educational opportunity'.[57] While this was often difficult to achieve in practice, he did not waver from wanting the Victorian state education system to advance towards this goal. He rejected equalising outcomes, retaining his sportsman's outlook on life. As someone who had made the most from his time at Caulfield Grammar, he doubtless wanted to give others the chance to excel. He condemned the practices of discouraging competition between students and ignoring the recognition of excellence, arguing that 'mediocrity flourishes' if such competitive endeavours were forgone.[58]

While his pedagogical views and teaching experience informed his decision-making, most of his challenges were structural and required more prosaic thinking. The demands on the Minister for Education came in all shapes and sizes. One of the first telegrams he received in the job came from Northcote Technical School. After offering their congratulations, the school representative asked him to investigate the failure to let a tender for a new toilet block. There were, however, some much larger, overarching issues that defined his tenure. The education system had been in crisis in the early 1950s as the first of the post-war baby boom children began their formal schooling. Thompson's predecessors had begun the immense task of physically expanding the system to accommodate the increased number of students. Nowhere was this seen more clearly than the number of new high schools constructed, 156 in total between 1954 and 1969.[59]

'Much has been done', Thompson wrote in 1967, adding 'much remains to be done.'[60] His primary task was to manage a system 'suffering from growing pains' by shepherding it through the peak of enrolments (see Table 1). Not only were more students entering the system, but they were staying in school for longer, as demonstrated by the number of students undertaking matriculation. In 1954, when he was teaching at Melbourne High School, Victoria had 4,178 candidates for matriculation. In 1967, that number was 22,869 – an increase far greater than the increase in the total secondary school pupil cohort.[61] This rapid growth, however, would not last forever. After hitting its peak in 1977, student numbers declined due to lower migration intakes, changing attitudes to family size and new birth control measures.[62] For the rest of the century, the total number of students in the system remained below 600,000.

Table 1: State primary and secondary education statistics, 1963-1985

Year	Schools	Primary and Secondary Students	Teachers
1963	2,233	469,840	19,041
1964	2,229	487,192	20,594
1965	2,232	504,120	21,899
1966	2,242	523,786	23,063
1967	2,241	540,281	24,373
1968	2,247	555,838	26,103
1969	2,235	572,125	27,957
1970	2,215	585,440	28,920
1971	2,197	593,933	30,212
1972	2,194	602,614	32,064
1973	2,179	605,644	34,215
1974	2,161	608,643	35,020
1975	2,161	618,112	37,728
1976	2,164	624,707	40,543
1977	2,162	626,317	41,895
1978	2,152	623,609	42,981
1979	2,155	614,419	40,779
1980	2,158	606,147	42,201
1981	2,149	595,042	41,769
1982	2,140	584,781	41,856
1983	2,124	582,034	42,895
1984	2,118	572,613	44,091
1985	2,118	558,764	44,907

Source: Victorian Year Books, 1963-1986.

Despite the significant effort since the 1950s to physically expand the system, moving into the 1970s, more schools and more classrooms were still required. Although Table 1 shows a decline in the number of schools over time, this is misleading. While more primary schools were closed over this period than were being built (see Table 2), they were usually small schools with an insufficient number of pupils to continue operating. The department continued to build new schools across the state to meet the increase in demand, as well as building new classrooms at existing schools. During the expansion period, the system required approximately 1,000 new classrooms each year just to keep pace.[63] Furthermore, existing facilities, particularly those belonging to older schools in inner metropolitan Melbourne, needed remodelling and rebuilding.[64] In any given year, therefore, the department was undertaking a considerable number of construction projects. In the 1970/71 financial year, for instance, in the primary division alone, the department established 17 new schools, replaced sub-standard classrooms in three schools, provided a replacement building of eight classrooms for Langwarrin Primary School, erected 506 new classrooms at existing schools and built 21 libraries and ten general-purpose rooms.[65]

Table 2: State primary schools established and closed, 1966-1975

Financial Year	Opened	Closed	Net Result
1966-1967	7 (plus three reopened)	11	-1
1967-1968	17	42	-25
1968-1969	11	17	-6
1969-1970	14	32	-18
1970-1971	17	51	-34
1971-1972	25	39	-14
1972-1973	13	19	-6
1973-1974	5	33	-23
1974-1975	15	30	-15

Source: Department of Education annual reports. Reporting becomes inconsistent after 1975.

Another significant challenge, corresponding with the expansion of high schools, was the need to recruit increasing numbers of qualified secondary school teachers. While Thompson found recruiting primary school teachers relatively easy, it was 'exceedingly difficult' to do the same for secondary schools, as each teacher required a three-year university degree followed by a Diploma of Education (a more stringent requirement than the qualifications needed to teach at primary-school level).[66] Indeed, he later noted that employing all the teachers required to fill every secondary school proved impossible.[67] Still, the department attempted to meet the demand. From approximately 12,000 secondary school teachers in the system in 1967, by 1975, there was close to 20,000.[68]

In addition to putting greater resources into recruiting efforts, Thompson also advocated for different solutions around easing the qualification requirements. This approach (and indeed many other decisions during this time) brought him into conflict with teachers' unions. These constant skirmishes formed another signature trials during his time as Minister for Education. In such a short book, it is impossible to catalogue every dispute between Thompson and one or more teachers' unions. For the sake of brevity, an example from 1969 is illustrative of this particular challenge.

Early in his tenure, Thompson gained acclaim for resolving some long-standing disputes between the Bolte Government and the VSTA, with Melbourne University political scientist Jean Holmes declaring that 'Victorian education is on the move at long last.'[69] To resolve some thorny issues, he had adopted a conciliatory approach, acceding to many of the union's requests. While this made for progress, it also led certain unions to believe that a militant approach had forced Thompson's hand, thus emboldening them to pursue a wider agenda.[70] In early 1969, their advocacy came into conflict with a scheme to address the shortage of secondary school teachers.

At that time, teacher numbers were static, with attrition taking teachers out of the system seemingly as quickly as they were being recruited; at the start of 1969 there were

852 freshly qualified secondary schools teachers entering the system, but by March 857 had departed through resignations or retirements. The department had developed two proposals to address the issue in the short-term. First, it would train 400 temporary teachers on a scheme that saw them teach for several days and then spend the remainder of the week at a secondary teaching college. Second, selected primary school teachers would take charge of junior secondary school mathematics.[71]

The VSTA opposed both measures, as each would involve under-qualified teachers working at secondary schools. They gave the department until 1 April to make more satisfactory arrangements, also demanding the right to determine whether the qualifications of a teacher entering any particular high school was adequate.[72] Thompson baulked at this latter suggestion, and the Director of Education, Fred Brooks, insisted that the measures proposed were the only means to ease pressure on secondary school staffing. The VSTA Secretary, Brian Conway, declared that they would not accept an 'anybody is better than nobody' attitude and, true to their word, began strike action when a young first-year primary school teacher, Barbara Wood, was appointed to teach mathematics at Noble Park High School. Thompson called the VSTA's attitude 'irresponsible' and condemned their strike action.[73] A parents' deputation urged him not to transfer Wood, as their children had indicated she was one of the better teachers at the school. Thompson personally spoke with her to ensure she was ready for the pressure inevitably coming from the VSTA. Confident that she had the sufficient 'mental strength', Thompson resolved to back her and the new policy.[74]

He dismissed the VSTA's alternative plan – which included putting teachers on full-time pay to undertake full-time study – as unrealistic, although he agreed to have this considered by the Teachers' Tribunal. Still, negotiations between Thompson and the VSTA stalled, and stop-work meetings continued through the middle months of 1969.[75] While Thompson publicly agreed with many of the VSTA's concerns, he countered that the only way to achieve what they wanted was to send children home from school until fully-trained teachers could be appointed – this he was not prepared to do. As such, he argued that there was no alternative but to implement short-term and imperfect remedies.[76]

The issue came to a head in October. After a 'pretty blonde art teacher' arrived at Northcote High School without the necessary qualifications, teachers went on strike within weeks of end-of-year exams.[77] To support the matriculation students left in limbo, Thompson arranged special coaching. Tackling the strike action itself, he threatened to stop the holiday pay for the teachers, as well as publicising the fact that eight of the striking teachers were themselves 'unqualified'. In a move towards conciliation, however, he announced improvements in the teacher trainees scheme (by 1972, humanities and science or mathematics teachers would have at least two years of tertiary education and teacher training). His action was decisive. On 17 November, the VSTA capitulated, ending a 45-day strike at the end of which they had gained nothing. It was, Jean Holmes wrote, a major victory for Thompson and 'a real feather in his cap'.[78] She would subsequently pronounce that his performance in the portfolio made him a strong contender for future party leadership.[79]

Conflict with teachers' unions was a constant feature of Thompson's time as Minister for Education. He was particularly condemnatory of strikes conducted in response to the shortage of secondary school teachers. The government recognised the shortage of teachers and the Education Department had a blank cheque to expand teacher training. Given the efforts he and the department were taking to address the issue, he labelled strike action in response to their proposals 'idiotic and incomprehensible'.[80] Still, as someone who both grew up in a family of teachers and worked as a teacher himself, he had greater empathy for the plight of teachers than some of his parliamentary colleagues. He was certainly more conciliatory than Bolte, who often used teachers' unions as a target to gain political mileage.[81]

Despite the notoriety he received throughout his political career for the perception that he was tough on unions, he recognised their role in protecting employees from unscrupulous employers and their important work preparing detailed cases to arbitration authorities for wage increases and improved conditions. He was, however, opposed to needless strike action that disrupted the public. In these instances, unions went from 'acting as the shield against victimisation to being the instigator of it'.[82] He also objected to the coercion and compulsion often associated with unions during that era, and he praised individual union members who rejected unreasonable directions of their leadership and acted, or so Thompson argued, in the interests of the greater good.

* * * *

It was during Lindsay Thompson's time as Minister for Education that the most dramatic moment of his political career occurred.[83] In the early afternoon of Friday 6 October 1972, Edwin Eastwood and Robert Boland kidnapped six pupils and their teacher, Mary Gibbs, from Faraday State School, a small, one-teacher school near Bendigo. The pair, both plasterers from Melbourne, had been inspired by the 1971 film *Dirty Harry*, and left a note at the school, demanding $1 million and stipulating that Thompson be the point of contact.

Once Victoria Police determined that the claims were genuine, Thompson and the then Premier, Dick Hamer, decided to pay the ransom to save hostages, despite the risk of setting a dangerous precedent. Early on Saturday morning, Thompson received his instructions: he was to be at Woodend Post Office at 5.00 am with the ransom money in a suitcase. Assistant Commissioner Mick Miller, who had phoned him to convey the demand, asked whether he was willing to undertake the task. Once Miller assured him that his action would likely secure the release of the hostages, Thompson agreed to go.

At 4.55 am, Thompson, Miller and Assistant Commissioner Bill Crowley arrived at the rendezvous location. Miller was concerned that the kidnappers would try to apprehend Thompson, and he remained armed in the backseat of their nearby car. Moving to the post office, Thompson vividly recalled the moment: 'I stood there in the rather eerie grey light which precedes the rising of the sun, rubbing my hands briskly to keep the blood circulating.'[84] Despite the appearance of a man who may or may not have been reconnoitring the post office to ensure that the minister had indeed arrived, there was no communication with the kidnappers. At 6.00 am, Thompson and his police escort went to Faraday School. There, they determined that it was likely a local was responsible for the kidnapping and set back to Melbourne to organise a search of the surrounding area.

On the way back to Melbourne, Miller woke a sleeping Thompson to inform him that Gibbs and her students had escaped from their kidnappers and were physically unharmed. Thompson, Miller and Crowley then headed to their location at Lancefield, where they met with Gibbs and her six pupils and learnt the details of their ordeal. The captives had managed to escape when Gibbs and the two oldest girls kicked their way out of the van in which they were being held and, after wandering through the bush, came upon a group of rabbit shooters who conveyed them to Lancefield. Gibbs was subsequently awarded the George Cross, while Boland and Eastwood were subsequently apprehended and convicted to 16 and 15 years' prison time respectively.

Thompson's actions during the Faraday kidnapping earned him significant praise, and he was awarded a Bronze Medal for Bravery from the Royal Humane Society. Yet this singular, dramatic event overshadowed the more mundane but no less important work he undertook for 12 years. Indeed, outside education circles, it seemed few appreciated his substantial achievements in such a difficult portfolio. When his tenure came to an end in 1979, political reporters were more interested in prognosticating about his chances of becoming the next Premier than assessing his legacy as the state's longest-serving Minister for Education. Similarly, history predominantly remembers Lindsay Thompson as the Education Minister willing to be the bagman at Woodend.

A sure-handed and thorough approach to managing an important portfolio does not quite capture the same headlines. Nevertheless, Thompson proved a very effective public administrator who oversaw significant change and reform (although too slowly for some of his detractors).[85] By 1979, the Education Department had 16,000 more teachers than had been in the case in 1967. Crucially, the increase in teachers was proportionally greater than the increase in students; the student/teacher ratio thus went from 22:1 to

15:1. His emphasis was not merely on numbers, however, and he was just as keen to commit resources to teacher training as he was to recruiting additional teachers into the system. He had also overseen the establishment of Deakin University (intended to establish tertiary education campuses outside Melbourne) and seen advances in the Victorian Institute of Colleges.

In 1969 he had published *Looking Ahead In Education*, a blueprint from the future of Victorian education, which he wrote in consultation with unions, teachers, parents, administrators and academics.[86] He made 65 recommendations covering each level of the education system. Most concerned administrative and structural matters, although some showed notable vision and ambition. 'Greater emphasis should be placed on developing an appreciation of the history, customs and language of the Asian people', he recommended.[87] There was no question in Thompson's mind that Australia's future was inextricably linked with Asia, and by 1978, 48 secondary schools were teaching Indonesian and 15 were teaching Japanese.[88] As a testament to the thought and consideration that went into *Looking Ahead In Education*, despite a change in government, by the 1990s the majority of his recommendations had been implemented.[89]

One of Thompson's major achievements was to reform the department itself, which he viewed as being far too centralised to be efficient. His proposal was to create regional headquarters where decisions could be made at a local level by those with a better understanding of local conditions and circumstances.[90] In 1969 he began the process to appoint three Assistant Directors-General of Education to restructure the department's senior administrative ranks, and in 1971 three regional directorates were established in Ballarat, Bendigo and Moe.[91] So great was the task of overhauling the department that he allegedly turned down on offer to move to a less-tempestuous portfolio in 1976 in order to see the reforms through to their end.[92] By the time he moved on, there were eleven regional directors acting as management agents for the department, as well as a marked increase in autonomy granted to schools for determining local administrative matters and educational policy in curriculum, techniques and experimentation. School councils and committees also had increased authority to carry out improvements and to employ ancillary staff.[93]

One series of reforms, of which his mother and grandmother would have been rightly proud, was his advocacy for gender equalisation within the department. When he was appointed, there were disparities between how married male and female teachers was handled. If a male studentship holder married, he was given an increase in his studentship allowance; if a female did the same, she was dismissed and required to pay back all the money she received in allowances and fee payments. Rightly appalled, in 1968, Thompson moved to abolish the 'archaic' practice. He also removed restrictions on fully-qualified married women without teaching experience being employed by the department and on married women undertaking teacher training courses.[94]

Another important reform concerned the ability of female teachers to be appointed school principals (which was only available at separate all-girls' schools). Despite years of distinguished service, his grandmother, Sarah Simpson, was denied the opportunity to become principal of Macarthur Street State School in Ballarat. In 1968, the first women were appointed as principals at mixed-sex secondary schools, and it gave Thompson personal satisfaction when, in 1970, the department abolished the restriction of women applying for primary school principal positions.[95] By the mid-1970s all the outdated restrictions limiting the employment and blocking the promotion of women, both married and single, had been abolished, and the Teachers' Tribunal had accepted and implemented the principle of equal pay for equal work.[96]

His time as Minister for Education was not without personal challenges. He and his family received death threats in the mail, often coinciding with a dispute with a teachers' union.[97] And by 1979, years in the demanding portfolio had worn him down. The man pictured inside the front cover of *Looking Ahead in Education*, who had energetically bounded into the portfolio, was now looking older than his 55 years. While he was still the same sharp-minded and physically strong individual, 12 years in such an arduous role had no doubt taken its toll on him.

Still, if Thompson had worked himself into the ground, it

was because he was responsible for an area of civic life that held deep significance for him. 'He eats, sleeps and drinks education', said his wife, Joan, in the mid-1970s, 'Why, we even finish up looking at a few schools every time we go out for a Sunday afternoon drive.'[98] His commitment to education imprinted itself on the mind of a generation of principals, teachers and administrators. Following his death, one high school principal wrote to his family: 'we felt we had an education minister who was prepared to go the extra mile for us. The school community admired him, many of whom felt they knew him well, and trusted him totally.'[99]

Hamer's deputy

In 1972, Henry Bolte, Victoria's imperious and long-serving Premier, resigned from office. His successor, Rupert 'Dick' Hamer, was a very different type of man with different priorities. Where Bolte was agricultural (in both background and disposition), the urbane Hamer came from Melbourne's affluent eastern suburbs. He also had a distinct vision for the state of Victoria, emphasising 'quality of life' issues such as the environment, the arts and heritage conservation.[100]

Lindsay Thompson, a man often talked about as a future Premier (but who was not known for his overt political ambition), had made a modest attempt to position himself as Bolte's successor. In advance of the 1970 election, he moved from the Legislative Council to the Legislative Assembly seat of Malvern (where he had been already living for 20 years).[101] The move was not well received by Bolte, however, who was allegedly displeased that Thompson had taken the step without his imprimatur. While some suggested that Bolte subsequently stymied Thompson's attempt to succeed him as Premier, it is more likely that he was simply not the man the party room preferred as Bolte's successor.[102]

Thompson was elected deputy leader, however. His main contender was Bill Borthwick, a cabinet minister since 1967 and a Deakinite liberal in the Hamer mould. Thompson did not canvass for votes, believing that his colleagues 'should know well the strengths and weaknesses of all possible candidates' already.[103] He defeated Borthwick after three ballots, leaving him surprised that the controversial education portfolio had not told against him.[104] Once elected, he offered Hamer his unqualified support and loyalty, deliberately seeking to emulate the close and productive working relationship between Bolte and Rylah. Not only did he believe this was appropriate, but he hoped to derive the same benefits for party cohesion and governmental effectiveness.[105] He described Hamer as 'a very good person with whom to work', noting his intelligence, work ethic and even temperament.[106] The pair developed an effective and close professional relationship and Thompson became 'as close a political friend as Hamer allowed'.[107]

Under Hamer, Thompson remained Minister for Education, benefitting from a slightly less turbulent period than during his early years in the portfolio. As Deputy Premier he now had a broader suite of responsibilities to consider. He was often required to be Acting Premier, as well as supporting Hamer at Premiers' meetings in Canberra. In his new role, he gained a broader perspective on the affairs of the state, mainly as they concerned relations with the Commonwealth. He never flinched from giving Hamer the public loyalty that he believed his leader deserved. Furthermore, he acted as an effective balance to Hamer, both in temperament (Thompson was notably warmer and more approachable than the often-aloof Hamer) and in focus. One historian noted that Thompson's 'keen interest and ability in budgetary matters, in particular his valued memory for statistics, proved a practical support to

Hamer's grand vision'.[108] The new-look Liberal government was a refreshing change for the state, and it comfortably won the 1973 election.

By now, Lindsay Thompson was one of the senior members of the government, widely known and respected for his avuncular attitude towards his parliamentary colleagues, irrespective of party affiliation. When Carl Kirkwood, the Labor member for Preston, gave his maiden speech in 1970, Thompson made him feel at home, letting him know that an opposition back-bencher had a job to perform for their electorate and that he would do whatever he could to assist.[109] One Christmas, the newly elected Country Party member for Rodney, Eddie Hann, sent Christmas greetings to the other members of parliament. Thompson returned the greeting, including a personal note that read: 'Congratulations, you are doing a good job.' 'There was no need for him to do that', Hann later reflected.[110] These were not isolated incidents, but were reflective of his general approach as a parliamentarian. Within his own party, he was particularly supportive of younger members, many of whom he actively mentored. At the 1973 election, 31-year-old Norman Lacy had been elected as the Liberal member for Warrandyte. Arriving with a strong interest in education, Thompson encouraged him in this area and they soon developed a close relationship. 'I was fortunate', Lacy later recalled, 'to fall into the hands of someone who became the most highly regarded member of that parliament.'[111]

Hamer's leadership continued to resonate with the electorate, and in 1976, his government was returned with an increased majority, holding 52 of 81 seats. He had only intended to serve for two full terms as Premier and that he would step down at some point before the next election. Yet several high-profile scandals soon engulfed his government, the most significant of which was the so-called 'land deals' affair, involving alleged ministerial impropriety regarding the purchase of land for future Housing Commission projects. With controversy growing, Hamer did not want his departure to be interpreted as a concession of defeat. He assumed the problems were temporary; he could ride them out and then retire on top on *his* terms, just as Bolte had done.[112]

Thompson never considered challenging Hamer for the leadership, whatever his ambitions may have been. Through his fourth term as Minister for Education from 1976 to 1979, he watched as the government became mired in controversy. The party's confident (and at times, over-confident) attitude after the 1976 election, Thompson wrote, was slowly being replaced by 'an atmosphere of tension and uncertainty'.[113]

While Hamer's leadership was beginning to falter, in 1977 Thompson featured in two prominent episodes while acting as Premier The first was a sequel to the harrowing events at Faraday. In late 1976, Edwin Eastwood escaped his incarceration on 14 February 1977 and proceeded to kidnap a teacher, Robert Hunter, and nine pupils from the one-teacher Wooreen Primary School in Gippsland. Eastwood abducted six more people and commandeered a Kombi van as he fled to a pre-prepared campsite for the evening. That night, one hostage, Robin Smith, managed to escape and alert the local police.

Early the next morning, Thompson and Assistant Commissioner Miller headed for Moorabbin airport to then fly to Gippsland as soon as possible. On the commute, Thompson determined that should the opportunity present itself he would exchange himself for the hostages. Fortunately this step was unnecessary. At dawn, Eastwood learnt of Smith's escape and made an abrupt departure. Police tracked the fleeing Kombi van with Thompson and Miller in a helicopter providing support. After breaking through two roadblocks on his way towards Sale, police stopped Eastwood at a third, and after a brief exchange of fire, he was arrested. He was subsequently sentenced concurrently with his previous sentence, effectively adding only three years to his non-parole period, and was released from prison in 1993. Thompson's role during the Wooreen kidnappings was more distant than at Faraday and did not capture the public imagination in the same way. Later in 1977, however, he would be right in the centre of critical events.

In 1967, government had approved the construction of a State Electricity Commission (SEC) gas-fired power station at Newport at the mouth of the Yarra River. Genuine environmental concerns, coupled with internal militant union politics, had seen work on the site delayed year upon year.[114] As public opinion turned in favour of construction and Hamer's negotiations with Trades Hall were stymied, the government established a diverse four-member panel to investigate the issues around the power station and hopefully be a circuit breaker to resolve the standoff.[115] The committee's final report was handed down on 5 May 1977, and despite suggesting some compromises to lessen the environmental impact it nevertheless recommended that construction commence (unless government could acquire a better site at a reasonable cost). The *Age* editorialised that all parties needed to abide by the arbitrators' verdict: 'The unions are honour-bound to withdraw their bans and let Newport be built without further argument and costly delay.'[116] Despite this, Trades Hall Council stubbornly refused to lift its ban on construction.[117]

The committee's decision coincided with Hamer's departure on a six-week tour of Europe, leaving Thompson to enact the government's response. In preparation for such an eventuality, the government had passed the *Vital State Projects Act* in 1976, which made it illegal to 'hinder or obstruct anything done or intended to be done in connection with a vital state project'. Now was the time to employ it. As the legislation governing the construction of the power plant needed to be amended to incorporate the committee's recommendations, Thompson and the cabinet took the opportunity to have Newport declared a vital state project. Advising Hamer of his intentions, Thompson recalled parliament on 11 May, and, after much rancorous debate, passed the necessary legislation. This action, to Thompson's mind, demonstrated that 'the government meant business'.[118]

Even still, legislative means alone could not advance the actual construction, and a defiant Trades Hall Council refused to back down. Undeterred, Thompson decided that construction should commence using volunteer labour. The SEC argued that this would be futile and that the government should put more pressure on the union movement, but Thompson retorted that three years of that approach had led nowhere. With cabinet agreement, the Public Works Department set about employing 21 tradesmen and a very apprehensive Thompson pondered whether he had made the right decision. On 23 May 1977, work recommenced at Newport with 16 men (five pulled out with second thoughts).[119]

To ensure effective on-site project management, Thompson called on a Public Works Department engineer, Jim Hicks, whom he knew to be effective from his work on several Education Department projects. Work proceeded, despite threats and obstruction from various militant unions. Some contractors feared that they would face retaliatory bans on other work sites because they were participating in the Newport project. There was only so much Thompson could do to help, but he gave them a guarantee that the government would do everything it could to ensure that other contracts were honoured. Despite the threats and bluster, the unions struggled to halt construction.

Work progressed steadily, and by 1980, Newport was connected to the SEC's electricity supply system. Thompson later described his actions during this critical stage of the long-running Newport sage as 'the biggest gamble' of his political life.[120] Newport was a personal triumph for the usually reserved Thompson, with many colleagues impressed by his decisiveness, compared with Hamer's prevarication.[121] Other cabinet ministers claimed credit for the solution to break the deadlock (it was a simple solution that multiple ministers might have developed independently), yet as Acting Premier, Thompson deserves the credit for its success, as he no doubt would have carried the responsibility had it failed.[122]

* * * *

By 1979, the Hamer Government was fraying at the edges. At the election that year the Liberal Party managed to retain government but lost 11 seats in the Legislative Assembly. There was a distinct air of decline for many on the treasury benches. In the post-election re-shuffle, Thompson finally left the education portfolio and became Chief Secretary and Treasurer, a sign, some believed, that Hamer was paving the way for Thompson to be his successor.[123] With many of the Chief Secretary's responsibilities since separated out to their own portfolios, the title was soon abolished, with its remaining responsibility, policing and emergency services, established as a ministry of its own. Thompson therefore became the first Minister for Police and Emergency Services and set about his new role with customary enthusiasm and attention to policy detail.[124]

He inherited the Treasury portfolio from the premier himself. Hamer had little interest in economics and while many commentators saw the handover as a way to prepare Thompson for the premiership, he was also likely relieved to be rid of a portfolio for which he had little enthusiasm.[125] This new responsibility was not merely a stepping stone, however, and Thompson was required to address the state's significant economic woes. Victoria had been struggling with high inflation, high unemployment and low growth since the end of the post-war economic boom in 1974, hampered, like all the states, by being in the shadow of the Commonwealth and subject to its powerful fiscal policy levers. Throughout the 1970s, decisions in Canberra often had a deleterious effect on Victoria: Gough Whitlam's 25 per cent tariff cut, for instance, had badly hurt Victoria's important manufacturing industry, while Malcolm Fraser's subsequent policy of 'fighting inflation first' did little to encourage much-needed economic growth.

Thompson's aim, as expressed in 1979 in his first budget, was to 'encourage city development and stability while keeping down inflation as much as possible'.[126] It was a difficult set of objectives to balance. He also sought a more proportionate slice of Commonwealth income tax revenue, giving the state government greater scope to implement job creation schemes. This continued to be a key aim. His second budget, handed down in September 1980, was described as a 'low alcohol document', which essentially put the state in a holding pattern until an income tax determination could be made (hopefully in Victoria's favour).[127] As Treasurer, Thompson tried to project a sense of confidence in the Victorian economy while still expressing concern about unemployment (a problem not unique to Victoria).[128]

By the start of the 1980s, Hamer had recognised that his 'quality of life' agenda (which had largely run its course anyway) needed to give way to a focus on economic management.[129] In December 1980 he released a policy document, 'New Directions for Economic Growth'. Its purpose, one commentator noted, was both 'to stimulate the flagging Victorian economy, and to improve the electoral prospects of the state government'.[130] The document was received poorly (due, mainly, to its brevity and lack of a substantive plan), and came to be a marker towards the premier's inauspicious denouement.[131]

At the start of 1981, Hamer confided to Thompson that he intended to retire in July or August that year, but events took the decision partially out of his hands.[132] One cabinet member, the Minister for Economic Development, Ian Smith, began causing issues for Hamer and was temporarily sacked from cabinet for breaking solidarity (with Thompson assisting the rapprochement).[133] In May 1981, Hamer left for the United States, and in his absence, Smith criticised Hamer to a reporter, with his remarks subsequently published on Saturday 23 May.[134] Thompson convened an informal meeting of the cabinet (*sans* Smith) at his home in Glen Iris the following morning to address the issue. They agreed that Smith's position was untenable, and that afternoon Thompson called him to demand his resignation. Smith agreed to comply, but only if he had a chance to inform the cabinet about his motivations and intentions for his remarks. Thompson agreed.[135]

Several other issues emerged concurrently to erode Hamer's leadership and he quickly flew back to Melbourne and met with Thompson to discuss the situation. By now, Hamer had decided to hand his resignation to the Governor. Thompson tried to convince him to stay, but he soon realised that his mind was made up, and Hamer announced his resignation on 28 May 1981.[136] During his statement, he remarked: 'I am grateful for the friendship and dedication of the Deputy Premier, Lindsay Thompson, over the whole period of premiership. No leader could have asked for more reliable or unstinted support.'[137] Thompson was ill-at-ease with the manner of Hamer's departure. 'He certainly deserved a better farewell week than the one he was obliged to endure in late May 1981', he wrote, 'a week characterised by criticism, ill feeling and disloyalty to his leadership.'[138]

On 2 June 1981, the parliamentary Liberal Party held a ballot to replace Hamer. Thompson and Borthwick were again the leading contenders. Both believed it was inappropriate to conduct leadership campaigns through the media and thought their colleagues knew their strengths and weaknesses well enough by now. Both also understood the challenge that the winner would face, primarily, the prospect of leading the Victorian Liberal Party to its first electoral defeat in 27 years. Nevertheless, Thompson did not wish to shirk that particular challenge. He won the ensuing ballot by a narrow margin, with Borthwick subsequently elected as deputy leader.[139]

Thompson's support seemingly came from the older members of the party room, those who believed that a loyal, capable, and decent man deserved his chance to lead.[140] The following day, the *Age* editorialised that it seemed appropriate that he should succeed Hamer, the longstanding minister having demonstrated that he was 'competent in administration and cool in a crisis'. The task before him, the *Age* noted, was 'not simply to survive politically but to lead the state towards a brighter future. We wish Mr Thompson well in the formidable tasks that face him.'[141]

Premier

Who was Lindsay Thompson, the man who would be the 40th Premier of Victoria? He had been a government mainstay for many years, and while not necessarily rising from obscurity, he was not one to seek public attention for the sake of his political aspirations or ego, often content to work hard in the background and leave the media spotlight to others. As such, many parts of the electorate were understandably curious about their new premier. In terms of external appearances, Thompson was tall, slight (frail some said), and possessed a 'lean and hungry look'.[142] The public came to know more about him over the coming months. In disposition, he was quiet and reserved, although never insecure or unsure of himself, as demonstrated by his fondness for self-effacing humour. He employed sporting metaphors generously, be they from football, cricket, tennis or golf, and they became part of his day-to-day language.

Politically he sat in the middle of the Liberal Party; he was neither staunch conservative nor Deakinite liberal. In fact, he disliked political labels entirely, subscribing to the view that 'people tend to differ on the issue raised'.[143] Socially conservative in his personal views and not a strong public advocate for Hamer's progressive reforms, he maintained his Menzies-style pragmatic liberalism. Rather than wanting to reshape society, he advanced practical policies that aimed to improve people's lives while extolling a set of moral ideals that emphasised the primacy of the individual. He believed in the rule of law and parliamentary government, and thought that the economy should be powered by free, private enterprise, with government intervention necessary to provide certain public services, overcome the effects of market failure and ensure a minimum standard of living for citizens.[144] These principles had guided his political career thus far, and would continue to do so during his time leading the state of Victoria.

On 5 June 1981, he was sworn in as Premier, also retaining his role as Treasurer. While honoured to be elected by the parliamentary party, he was under no illusions as to the challenge before him. The public's perception of the government was not positive. After 26 years, the Liberal government seemed tired, bereft of energy and new ideas and plagued with scandals, indecision and internal instability. 'It was obvious', he later wrote, 'that a tremendous effort would be needed to save [the party] from defeat in the 1982 election poll.'[145]

The 1979 election reduced the government's lower house majority to nine seats: the Liberal Party held 41, Labor held 32, with the Country Party in possession of eight. A private poll conducted in July and August 1981 showed the state of play with regards to voter intentions at the next election: Liberal Party 31 per cent, National Party five per cent, ALP 53 per cent and Australian Democrats seven per cent.[146] Many within the Liberal Party hoped Thompson could reinvigorate the government before the next election, although some were concerned that as Hamer's deputy he would be seen as merely 'more of the same'. Furthermore, Labor considered him to be the least formidable of the men who could have replaced Hamer.[147]

Thompson's period as Premier was predominantly defined by the issues before him – he did not have the opportunity to articulate and enact a sweeping agenda as Bolte and Hamer had done. He continued the work done during the Hamer years of trying to streamline government operations and reduce expenditure, but the key focus for the Thompson Government would be the economy.[148] Victorian manufacturing was in terminal decline; tariff protection kept the industry afloat, but only just, with the industry losing jobs at an alarming rate.[149] The 'New Directions' policy, thin as it was, had been a step in the right direction, even if it was overshadowed by the turmoil of Hamer's final months. Thompson continued to aim to encourage economic growth and gain more of its income tax back from Canberra (which could then be used for public sector stimulus). He even produced a booklet, *A Fair Deal For Victoria*, replete with tables and coloured charts to help make his case at home and abroad.[150]

While economic development was a high priority for the government, industrial relations issues were still prevalent. Among several high-profile industrial disputes during Thompson's time as Premier, the Transport Workers' Union (TWU) strike in July 1981 was the most prominent. At the start of the month the TWU called a strike in favour of a $20 per week pay rise. Whatever the merits of their claim, they made a significant tactical error by failing to exempt milk deliveries from the dispute. When the strike began on 15 July, it applied to all types of deliveries, with no exceptions made for hospitals, pregnant mothers or young babies. The action was quickly condemned by the government and most media outlets. Thompson determined that the 'irresponsible unionists had reached the limit'.[151] He was not prepared to negotiate with the TWU while it denied milk to vulnerable Victorians. As such, he felt that using the *Essential Services Act* to force the TWU to comply was not only justified but necessary.

Together with Borthwick, he set to work organising a replacement service for milk delivery and distribution. Some 20 tonnes of milk powder was procured from a factory in Dandenong, with trucks for its distribution operated by volunteers from the State Emergency Service. On 21 July, the government invoked the *Essential Services Act* and declared a state of emergency. The government-procured trucks, with a police escort, commenced their deliveries.[152] Several days later, they used the same approach to ensure that retailers received basic foods. The Victorian Secretary of the TWU, Jim Davis (whom Thompson described as a reasonable man), soon met with the Premier and agreed, without reservations, to recommence deliveries.[153] The dispute ended on 28 July in the government's favour.[154]

His handling of the strike allowed him to be the confident and decisive leader the parliamentary party was probably looking for when they elected him. His decision to invoke the *Essential Services Act* was portrayed – positively – as most un-Hamer-like and put the ALP on the back foot for the first time in many months.[155] Thompson had several other successes from adopting a decisive approach to dealing with issues, earning him an increased personal approval rating against the opposition leader, Frank Wilkes.[156] Some suggested that he take the opportunity to call an early election, but he swatted aside such notions, not wanting to engage in flagrant political opportunism.[157] Bob Hawke, then the federal member for Wills in northern Melbourne, believed that if the Liberal Party were ever going to win the next election, it should have called it during the TWU dispute – but Thompson was far too decent to think that way.[158]

The parliamentary session of late 1981 (the only session of Thompson's period as Premier), was an opportunity to challenge the public perception that the government was fatigued and divisive. Unfortunately for Thompson, the results were mixed. The Legislative Assembly sat for a record 42 days from 8 September to 22 December, passing 150 bills, with 20 remaining uncompleted.[159] Much of the legislation advanced progressive but unspectacular reforms that failed to capture the public's imagination.[160] The most significant success, certainly in Thompson's estimation, was the passage of the *Wrongs (Public Contracts) Act*.[161] The legislation enabled the government and state-run organisations (such as the SEC) to sue trade unions for damages caused as a result of industrial action, allowing them to combat what Thompson later called 'irresponsible unionism'.[162] Although condemned by the Labor Party, the new legislation was effective in seeing the Builders' Labourers' Federation lift bans on the new Loy Yang power station in the Latrobe Valley.[163]

Other legislative moves were not successful. In July, the Liberal Party's state council had called on the government to abandon all restrictions on shopping hours, a move supported by large inner-city retailers but opposed by the Shop Assistants' Union and small retailers. On 14 October, Thompson announced that, as a trial, retailers could trade until 6.00 pm on the four Saturdays leading up to Christmas. Unfortunately for the Premier, opposition in his backbench publicly forced him to reverse the policy. This small issue became magnified by the government's standing in the polls, reinforcing the idea of a divided party room. The opposition relished the opportunity to criticise Thompson and his government, and, as one commentator noted, 'the incident did nothing to enhance Thompson's much cultivated reputation for decisiveness and leadership'.[164]

Thompson's fortunes as premier turned decisively on 8 September, when the ALP caucus elected John Cain junior to lead the parliamentary party. Until then, Thompson had contended against the ineffectual Frank Wilkes. Now he was facing an invigorated opponent. Only seven years his junior, Cain brought fresh energy to the opposition. After the promising 1979 election result, Victoria's economic downturn and the internal Liberal Party conflagration, he believed the Labor Party was closer than it had been in 27 years to returning to government. At the start of 1982, Liberal Party strategists debated whether to go to the polls early or wait as long as possible, hoping that some calamity would befall the opposition. Thompson settled this question on 10 February, when he announced a 3 April election, a decision he had mainly kept to himself.[165]

The economy emerged as the central issue of the campaign.[166] Thompson argued that only the Liberal Party could provide the state with sound economic management, and he highlighted the party's successes of the past 27 years.[167] He tried to demonstrate that the ALP's vast array of pre-election promises were unrealistic, an attempt to undermine their credibility as potential economic managers.[168] For his part, Thompson did not want to commit to un-costed policy for the sake of improving his electoral prospects. He believed such an approach to be 'irresponsible and typify the manner of policy decision-making which so often brings politicians into contempt'.[169] As he noted in his policy speech on 10 March, he was unprepared to promise 'the sun, moon and stars', because 'we couldn't afford them anyway'.[170]

In contravention of standard practice, Thompson accepted Cain's invitations to formal leaders' debates during the campaign. He knew he needed to make up ground, and this was a way to do it.[171] While the substance of the debates mattered little to the eventual election outcome, Cain looked much younger and considerably fresher than Thompson. One historian noted that 'Thompson's thin face, etched even deeper with the exhaustion of fighting a losing campaign and calming his anxious team, encapsulated the view that the Liberals were old and tired'.[172] Late in the campaign, he was clearly instructed to take a more aggressive approach in these debates, which ultimately proved ineffective.[173] Despite this, he refrained from personal attacks directed at Cain, as some advisers were encouraging him to do. 'It seemed to me', he later wrote, 'that if the only way we could win an election was by using personal abuse then we must be going badly.'[174]

For all Thompson's efforts, overcoming the party's myriad issues was a bridge too far. While some party members later expressed the opinion that Bill Borthwick might have offered a better chance of retaining government, it is doubtful that he – or anyone else – could have changed the party's fortunes.[175] The electorate believed that after 27 years of Liberal government it was time for a change. On 3 April, Victoria overwhelmingly voted for the ALP for the first time since 1952. The Liberal Party lost 17 seats in the Legislative Assembly, with Labor now holding 49 of 81 seats. The hardest blow fell on many talented and industrious Liberal members who lost their seats in the landslide. If the loss was inevitable, it was no less sad for those doing the losing. Few saw Thompson arrive at the Royal Exhibition Building tally room late that evening, and after talking with John Cain and several colleagues who had lost their seats (which included

Borthwick), he looked to depart. On his way out, Dick Hamer put an arm around his loyal deputy's shoulders as they walked together to the exit.[176]

Later life and legacy

Thompson blamed no-one but himself for the election defeat, making a comparison to the way a football coach would take responsibility for a poor loss. The following day he told the press that he felt like 'Tom Hafey explaining why Collingwood has not won another grand final'.[177] He believed the challenge of leading the Liberal Party back to government belonged to the next generation and after a period of reorganisation and consolidation he resigned from Victorian Parliament. The 34-year-old Jeffrey Kennett was elected opposition leader in his place. The bi-partisan tributes offered to him on his final day in parliament moved him greatly. Addressing the Legislative Assembly for the final time, he thanked the other members for their warm valedictory remarks, acknowledged the service of his personal staff and expressed his appreciation at having the privilege to serve in parliament for so long. With that, he declared that it was now an appropriate time to be 'heading for the pavilion'.[178]

Despite his resignation, the 59-year-old still had many years to commit to public service. For the first time since 1955, however, this would need to be conducted exclusively away from Spring Street. Among the many trusts and committees that benefited from his wealth of parliamentary experience, sport and recreation remained a key passion. In addition to prominent roles with the Victorian Cricket Association, the National Tennis Centre Trust and the Royal Life Saving Society Australia, in 1987 he was elected chairman of the Melbourne

Cricket Ground Trust (having been a trustee since 1967) and he oversaw the construction of the ground's Great Southern Stand. His love of football, and the Richmond Football Club in particular, did not abate, and in 1999 the club invited him to be on the committee to select its 'team of the century'.

In the late 1980s, he commenced a project few former state premiers ever attempted: writing his memoirs. *I Remember: An Autobiography* was published in 1989. Dense in policy detail, it re-litigated many of the critical decisions he had made over his political career and provided detailed accounts of the kidnappings at Faraday and Wooreen. It was replete with humorous anecdotes (often at his own expense) and devoid of the type of score-settling that permeates most contemporary political autobiographies. Geoffrey Blainey, who had been at the University of Melbourne with Thompson, wrote the foreword, observing that his recollections reflected both his fairness and firmness. The book was dedicated to his wife and family, 'in appreciation of their loyal support, encouragement and tolerance of the many interruptions to home life over three decades'.

His post-politics commitments slowly wound down as the years passed. He spent his time playing golf for the exercise and competition, doing crosswords to keep himself mentally sharp and corresponding with the multitude of friends, former colleagues and acquaintances he had met throughout his life. In 1998, the Victorian government established the Lindsay Thompson Fellowship, awarded to assist the professional development of state school teachers. Each year, without fail, he personally presented the fellowship to its recipient at the education excellence awards ceremony, always regaling the audience with a humorous speech. In 1990, he had delivered the eulogy at Henry Bolte's state funeral, and in March 2004, he did the same following Dick Hamer's death. Although looking frail, his remarks were delivered with power, precision and without notes, demonstrating that he had lost none of his oratorical skill.

Lindsay Thompson's health rapidly declined, and he died on 16 July 2008, suffering pneumonia, aged 84. At a state funeral held at St Paul's Cathedral, Melbourne, former colleagues and opponents gathered along with family, friends and other mourners to pay their respects to Victoria's longest-serving cabinet member. The Saturday after his death, Richmond wore black armbands to acknowledge the passing of their former number one ticket holder and defeated Essendon at the MCG by four points.

Several days later, Victorian Parliament reconvened on the afternoon of Tuesday, 29 July, to give members the chance to offer their own tributes. One after the other, government and opposition members rose to offer their condolences and praise Lindsay Thompson's legacy. After thirteen speakers, the final remarks were left to the member for Sandringham, Murray Thompson. Lindsay's eldest son had followed his father into parliament, and he offered some reflections and publicly thanked those who had cared for his father in his final years. In his concluding remarks, Murray noted: 'It may well be said in the words of St Paul that my father, with rare distinction, fought the good fight, finished the race and kept the faith'.[179]

* * * *

Lindsay Thompson's life and career are far more extensive than have been presented here. The essence of this book, however, was to address the simple question raised in the introduction: how was it that Lindsay Thompson managed to maintain such an esteemed reputation as a parliamentarian throughout his long career? His attributes as a politician have been readily described throughout this book, with two broad themes emerging prominently.

First, within in an environment that often lends itself to conflict and rivalry, that presents opportunities for corruption and sharp practice and that often corrodes moral decision making, Lindsay Thompson was steadfast in maintaining an upright and honourable character. The Leader of the National Party, Peter Ross-Edwards, described him as 'a gentleman and a sportsman', a succinct way to encapsulate a variety of attributes.[180] He was lauded for his integrity, selflessness (particularly his dedication to serving the state) and for never having a cross word to say about anyone. He never betrayed his deeply-held principles, he was unceasingly loyal to both people and institutions, and he maintained an almost old-fashioned sense of fairness, no doubt derived from an idealised version of how be believed sport should be played. He also possessed a quiet courage and an ability to remain calm under pressure – amply demonstrated by his actions during the Faraday kidnapping.

He was also courteous, warm towards even the most casual of acquaintances, approachable to strangers and particularly welcoming to new members of parliament. He could remember details about people, not merely recalling their names, but being able to ask about family members or specific circumstances an interlocutor may have mentioned on an earlier occasion. The warmth and genuineness of his interpersonal relationships with his parliamentary colleagues was a chief reason he was held in such high regard, at least by those with whom he served. Neil Trezise, a minister in John Cain's Government, noted: 'I have never heard ... one single word being said against Lindsay, because I would not believe one single word against him, in regard to his personal qualities. He is perhaps the fairest man one could meet wherever one went in whatever walk of life.'[181]

He managed to maintain his integrity and decency because he took seriously the moral qualities espoused during his formative years, which were then reinforced throughout his life through regular attendance at his local church. He also earnestly believed in democracy as the best form of government and knew that if parliaments were to function at their best then elected representatives needed to reject the baser instincts that so often undermine the democratic project.

Extolling his virtues, however, does not mean that he lacked some less sociable qualities sometimes needed for governing. While he was often prepared to be a peacemaker, either within the party or externally with his political opponents, he was not prepared to countenance any action he deemed coercive or any argument he considered unreasonable or unsubstantiated. Unlike the genteel Hamer, Thompson was always a sportsman, and understood the nature of the contest. His sporting metaphors were not merely illustrative, they betrayed a deep understanding that politics, as with sport, was a contest to be fought and won. While never stooping to levels he judged unworthy of public office, he was prepared to fight hard when he believed he was in the right and, importantly, could argue such to the public. Furthermore, Thompson always played the ball, never the man. As one opposition member noted, 'no matter how tenaciously, bitterly and strenuously he fought for his principles, with which I quite often disagreed, he always fought fairly … he always fought in terms of principle and he never disintegrated into either personal character assassination or personal abuse.'[182]

Second, he was an exceedingly competent Minister of the Crown. With the capacity for 'calm judgement and focused action', he was an efficient administrator, an effective debater and was committed to understanding policy detail.[183] 'He really thought through policy issues', reflected John Cain, 'They don't breed 'em like that any more.'[184] He possessed many favourable and useful attributes that helped in the execution of his duties, foremost of which was his prodigious work ethic (an attribute, Cain argued, that was essential for success in parliament).[185] Furthermore, it was said that he had 'an eye for detail, a head for statistics and the memory of an elephant'.[186] He had also learned very early in his career the benefit of gaining hands-on knowledge to assist his decision making.

He also favoured practicality over ideology and was prepared to change his views based on evidence. On the long-standing and high-profile issue of capital punishment, he came into parliament as a retentionist, arguing that it was 'an appropriate form of punishment for certain types of murder', based on evidence suggesting that it was an effective deterrent.[187] By 1975, when Hamer introduced his Private Member's Bill abolishing capital punishment, Thompson's position had changed. After an 'exhaustive survey of all the evidence available in the Library', he informed the Legislative Assembly, he had concluded that 'there is no detectable relationship between the retention of capital punishment and the murder rates in a nation or in a State'.[188] All his attributes as a parliamentarian made him the type of daunting and dogged political opponent he himself had found imposing as a young member of the Legislative Council.

He also never ceased being a teacher. He actively mentored and supported younger colleagues and often went to great effort to explain the rationale behind his decisions, be it to other cabinet members, parliamentary colleagues or the general public, and could communicate and translate complex topics into language the average voter would readily understand (usually through sporting metaphors). As Treasurer, for instance, he devoted considerable time to ensuring all members of parliament had a better understanding of the opaque processes involved in the budget.[189] His three publications while in parliament, *Victorian Housing, Today and Tomorrow*, *Looking Ahead in Education* and *A Fair Deal for Victoria*, were all attempts to shed light on complex public policy issues for the benefit of the general public.

Lindsay Thompson's attributes as a parliamentarian are clearly laudable. Yet it is worth noting that he was not elected to succeed Bolte in 1972, nor did his support when elected to deputy leader – or indeed when he was later elected leader – come from an overwhelming majority of his parliamentary colleagues. Factional and electoral considerations were no doubt at play in the party room's thinking, yet it is clear that despite his acknowledged strengths as a minister, he was not necessarily considered the best fit for party leadership at the times when that question was being put. Specific critiques of Thompson as a parliamentarian, however, are difficult to find. No doubt union officials and other opponents had choice words about him during any number of the battles in which he played a leading role. When pressed, one might say that while decisive in moments of crisis, he was more cautious when it came to matters of reform. He was not noted as a big-picture thinker in the same mould as Hamer, preferring to master details rather than present a grand vision for reshaping society. In addition, while he had arrived in parliament with energy and enthusiasm, the burden of difficult portfolios had worn him down over time, such that by the late 1970s he was seen as less charismatic than many of his colleagues. None of this made him any less of a parliamentarian, but they provided a point of difference in a party room deciding on their future leadership.

Adverse observations about him usually came from those outside parliament, and mainly concerned how he was viewed externally, where many of his strengths were often hidden behind his reserved personality. Upon his election as Premier, one reporter described him as 'a gaunt man, a shadowy figure, a politician who needs a little more charisma – and a new tailor.'[190] His ministerial performance was once uncharitably described as 'pedestrian', a judgement likely made by those unable to see the tremendous volume of work he undertook as a parliamentarian or who had not engaged with him directly on a matter of policy.[191] During the 1982 election campaign, several colleagues and observers, out of frustration more than malice, believed that he struggled to project his impressive personal qualities to the broader public. Liberal Party officials called him 'a strong man on the quiet', a fitting description of Lindsay Thompson, but not one that seemed to resonate with voters when it mattered.[192] Still, he had spent his parliamentary career valuing substance over style, and to reinvent himself overnight simply for the sake of seeking electoral advantage would have been unbecoming and completely out of character.

Finally, it is important to recognise, as Thompson perfectly understood, that his success did not arrive merely from an application of individual effort. First, governmental effectiveness was a team game. When being lauded for his achievements upon his retirement, he noted that nearly all were the product of a team effort and many were initially suggested by colleagues.[193] Second, the longevity of his political career owed as much to his impeccable timing as it did to his character and competence. Elected to parliament in 1955, he was a beneficiary of the ALP Split, which made organised and united opposition to the Liberal government difficult for several decades. He also avoided a prolonged period in opposition, where he might not have thrived or he may have been unable to maintain his high standards of decency in a more confrontational role. Still, although circumstances outside his control gave him the opportunity for a long and successful career, it required a tremendous personal and professional investment to work to the consistently high standard that he demanded of himself and for which the public benefited.

Lindsay Thompson began his memoirs by referring to his grandmother, noting that she belonged to a world that had vanished. We may well say the same of him. He was of a time when parliamentarians were held in (slightly) higher regard than is the case in the twenty-first century. Thompson's party colleague, Walter Jona, believed that in the 1960s most elected representatives 'saw themselves as parliamentarians rather than just politicians and, as a consequence, enjoyed much greater respect from the community than that which the parliament earns today'.[194] Anecdotally, it also seems that the majority of Thompson's time in parliament was spent in a much more civil and collegial environment than is the case today.

Given the manner in which party politics has changed since then, it perhaps unreasonable to hope that any modern politician could emulate his approach. It is highly unlikely that simply being decent and capable is sufficient to see someone rise to the top of a political party. Still, if there was no place in contemporary legislatures for the virtues that defined Lindsay Thompson's career of public service, then the health of Australian democracy would be all the poorer for it.

1   *Victorian Parliamentary Debates* (hereafter *VPD*) Legislative Assembly (LA), 4 November 1982, pp. 1611-12.

2   Lindsay H. Thompson, *I Remember: An Autobiography*, Hyland House, Melbourne, 1989, p. 235.

3   *VPD* (LA), 4 November 1982, p. 1613.

4   Ibid., p. 1626.

5   Ibid., p. 1617.

6   Thompson, *I Remember*, p. 1.

7   Judith Brett, *Australian Liberals and the Moral Middle Class*, Cambridge University Press, Cambridge, 2003, p. 9.

8   Lindsay. H. Thompson, *Looking Ahead in Education*, Department of Education, Melbourne, 1969, pp. 5-6.

9   Brett, *Australian Liberals*, p. 11.

10 Thompson, *I Remember*, p. 6; *Age*, 12 December 1941.

11 Thompson, *I Remember*, p. 6.

12 *VPD* (LA), 4 November 1982, p. 1630.

13 Thompson, *I Remember*, p. 17.

14 *Age*, 27 June 1979.

15 Thompson, *I Remember*, pp. 21-22.

16 Thompson, *Looking Ahead in Education*, p. 1.

17 Speech to the NSW Labor Party Conference, 12 June 1949.

18 Thompson, *I Remember*, p. 44.

19 *Argus*, 17 October 1944.

20 Speech, 'The Forgotten People', 22 May 1942.

21 Brett, *Australian Liberals*, p. 35.

22 Thompson, *I Remember*, pp. 14-16.

23 Ibid., p. 25.

24 Ibid., pp. 25-26.

25 *Argus*, 31 January 1955.

26   Thompson, *I Remember*, p. 31.

27   Ibid., p. 33.

28   *VPD*, 16 June 1955, p. 37. Until September 1982, Hansards were not separated between Legislative Assembly and Legislative Council volumes.

29   *VPD*, 16 June 1955, p. 37.

30   Ibid., p. 37.

31   Thompson, *I Remember*, p. 31.

32   Ibid., p. 52.

33   *VPD* (LA), 4 November 1982, p. 1612.

34   Anne Tiernan and Patrick Weller, *Learning to Be a Minister: Heroic Expectations, Practical Realities*, Melbourne University Press, Carlton, 2010, pp. 1-2.

35   Thompson, *I Remember*, p. 72.

36   Ibid., pp. 72-76.

37   Ibid., p. 59.

38   Ibid., p. 59.

39   Bree Carlton, '"Machine Living": The Discourses and Ideologies of Spatial Order Which Informed the High Rise Developments of the Housing Commission Victoria 1950-1970', *Melbourne Historical Journal*, Vol. 27, No. 1, 1999, p. 101.

40   Thompson, *I Remember*, pp. 61-62.

41   Ibid., p. 62.

42   Ibid., pp. 62-63.

43   Alan Vaarwerk, 'Suburbs in the Sky: High-rise commission flats and the Melbourne imagination', *Kill Your Darlings* website, 4 May 2016, https://www.killyourdarlings.com.au/2016/05/suburbs-in-the-sky-high-rise-commission-flats-and-the-melbourne-imagination/, accessed 30 April 2020.

44   Carlton, "Machine Living", p. 100.

45   Vaarwerk, 'Suburbs in the Sky'.

46   Thompson, *I Remember*, p. 60.

47   Ibid., p. 65.

48   V.H. Arnold, *Victorian Year Book 1967 No. 81*, Commonwealth Bureau of Census and Statistics,

Melbourne, 1967, p. 461.

49   *VPD*, 13 September 1967, pp. 102-06.

50   V.H. Arnold, *Victorian Year Book 1969 No. 83*, Commonwealth Bureau of Census and Statistics, Melbourne, 1969, p. 482.

51   Arnold, *Victorian Year Book 1967*, p. 461.

52   Department of Education, *Report of the Minister of Education for the Year 1968-69*, C.H. Rixon, Government Printer, Melbourne, 1970, p. 5.

53   Arnold, *Victorian Year Book 1969*, p. 482.

54   Arnold, *Victorian Year Book 1967*, p. 464.

55   *Argus*, 5 February 1955.

56   Department of Education, *Report of the Minister of Education for the Year 1970-71*, C.H. Rixon, Government Printer, Melbourne, 1972, p. 5.

57   Thompson, *Looking Ahead in Education*, pp. 4-5.

58   Thompson, *I Remember*, p. 112.

59   Ibid., p. 85.

60   Department of Education, *Report of the Minister of Education for the Year 1966-67*, A.C. Brooks, Government Printer, Melbourne, 1968, p. 1.

61   V.H. Arnold, *Victorian Year-Book 1952-53 and 1953-54 No. 73*, A.C. Brooks, Government Printer, Melbourne, 1954, pp. 251, 265; Arnold, *Victorian Year Book 1969*, pp. 482, 498.

62   Thompson, *I Remember*, p. 89.

63   Ibid., p. 89.

64   *Age*, 8 February 1971.

65   Department of Education, *Report of the Minister of Education for the Year 1970-71*, p. 6.

66   Thompson, *I Remember*, pp. 89-90.

67   Ibid., p. 85.

68   Arnold, *Victorian Year Book 1969*, p. 482; N. Bowden, *Victorian Year Book 1976 No. 90*, Australian Bureau of Statistics, Melbourne, 1976, p. 645.

69   'Australian Political Chronicle January-April 1968', *Australian Journal of Politics and History* (hereafter *AJPH*), Vol. 14, Issue 2, August 1968, p. 256.

70   Thompson, *I Remember*, p. 91.

71   *Age*, 28 April 1969.

72   Thompson, *I Remember*, p. 91.

73   'Australian Political Chronicle January-April 1969', *AJPH*, Vol. 15, Issue 2, August 1969, p. 93.

74   Thompson, *I Remember*, p. 91.

75   'Australian Political Chronicle January-April 1969', p. 93; *Age*, 24 July 1969.

76   'Australian Political Chronicle May-August 1969', *AJPH*, Vol. 15, Issue 3, December 1969, p. 97.

77   'Australian Political Chronicle September-December 1969', *AJPH*, Vol. 16, No. 1, April 1970, p. 88.

78   Ibid., p. 88.

79   'Australian Political Chronicle January-April 1970', *AJPH*, Vol. 16, Issue 2, August 1970, p. 246.

80   Thompson, *I Remember*, p. 92.

81   Peter Blazey, *Bolte: A Political Biography*, The Jacaranda Press, Milton, 1972, p. 220.

82   Thompson, *I Remember*, pp. 223-24.

83   A detailed account of both the Faraday and the subsequent Wooreen kidnappings can be found in *I Remember*, pp. 161-81.

84   Thompson, *I Remember*, p. 164.

85   *Age*, 29 May 1981.

86   Thompson, *I Remember*, p. 92.

87   Thompson, *Looking Ahead In Education*, p. 94.

88   Thompson, *I Remember*, p. 101.

89   *VPD* (LA), 29 July 2008, p. 2705.

90   Thompson, *I Remember*, p. 93.

91   *VPD*, 1 May 1969, pp. 4401; Department of Education, *Report of the Minister of Education for the Year 1972-73*, C.H. Rixon, Government Printer, Melbourne, 1973, p. 4.

92   *Age*, 29 May 1981.

93   I.M. Cowie, *Victoria Year Book 1980 Number 94*, Australian Bureau of Statistics, Melbourne, 1980, pp. 574-75.

94   Thompson, *I Remember*, pp. 104-05.

95   Ibid., p. 105.

96   Ibid., pp. 104-05.

97   Ibid., p. 101.

98   *Age*, 29 May 1981.

99   Quoted in *VPD* (LA), 29 July 2008, p. 2710.

100   'Australian Political Chronicle May-August 1972', *AJPH*,
        Vol. 18, Issue 3, December 1972, p. 420; Thompson, *I
        Remember*, p. 121.

101   Thompson, *I Remember*, p. 118.

102   Colebatch, *Dick Hamer*, p. 190; Blazey, *Bolte*, p. 221;
        Thompson, *I Remember*, p. 119.

103   Thompson, *I Remember*, p. 119.

104   Ibid., p. 120.

105   Ibid., pp. 34, 120.

106   Ibid., p. 34.

107   Colebatch, *Dick Hamer*, p. 394.

108   Victoria Peel, 'Lindsay Thompson: The team players',
        in Paul Strangio and Brian Costar (eds), *The Victorian
        Premiers 1856-2006*, Federation Press, Annandale, 2006,
        p. 317.

109   *VPD* (LA), 4 November 1982, p. 1624.

110   Ibid., p. 1618.

111   Interview with Norman Lacy, 28 September 2017.

112   Colebatch, *Dick Hamer*, pp. 306-07, 380.

113   Thompson, *I Remember*, p. 132.

114   'Australian Political Chronicle July-December 1976',
        AJPH, Vol. 23, Issue 1, April 1977, p. 86.

115   Colebatch, *Dick Hamer*, p. 291.

116   *Age*, 29 April 1977.

117   Thompson, *I Remember*, p. 185.

118   Ibid., pp. 186-87.

119   Ibid., p. 190.

120   Ibid., p. 182.

121   Colebatch, *Dick Hamer*, p. 294.

122   Ibid., p. 292.

123   *Age*, 19 May 1979.

124   Thompson, *I Remember*, p. 199.

125   Colebatch, *Dick Hamer*, pp. 315-16; 'Australian Political
        Chronicle January-June 1979', *AJPH*, Vol. 25, Issue 3,

December 1979, p. 401.

126   'Australian Political Chronicle July-December 1979', *AJPH*, Vol. 26, Issue 1, April 1980, p. 124.

127   *Age*, 18 September 1980.

128   *VPD*, 17 September 1980, p. 527.

129   Colebatch, *Dick Hamer*, p. 383.

130   'Australian Political Chronicle July-December 1980', *AJPH*, Vol. 27, Issue 1, April 1981, p. 87.

131   Colebatch, *Dick Hamer*, pp. 392-93.

132   Ibid., p. 394.

133   Thompson, *I Remember*, p. 203; Colebatch, *Dick Hamer*, p. 396.

134   Colebatch, *Dick Hamer*, p. 403.

135   Thompson, *I Remember*, p. 204.

136   Ibid., p. 205.

137   Statement upon his resignation, 28 May 1981.

138   Thompson, *I Remember*, p. 206.

139   Ibid., pp. 207-08.

140   Colebatch, *Dick Hamer*, p. 409.

141   *Age*, 3 June 1981.

142   *Age*, 18 July 2008.

143   *Age*, 27 June 1979.

144   Waleed Aly, 'What's Right? The Future of Conservatism in Australia', *Quarterly Essay*, Issue 37, 2020, p. 25.

145   Thompson, *I Remember*, pp. 208-9.

146   Kevin Foley, 'The Liberal Party Campaign', in Brian J. Costar and Colin A. Hughes (eds.), *Labour To Office: The Victorian State Election 1982*, Drummond, Blackburn, 1983, p. 37.

147   *Age*, 18 June 1981.

148   Thompson, *I Remember*, p. 218.

149   Brian J. Costar and Colin A. Hughes, 'Introduction', in Costar and Hughes, *Labor To Office*, p. x.

150   Lindsay.H. Thompson, *A Fair Deal For Victoria*, Government Printer, Melbourne, 1981.

151   'Australian Political Chronicle July-December 1981', *AJPH*, Vol. 28, Issue 1, April 1982, p. 103; Thompson, *I Remember*, p. 211.

152 Thompson, *I Remember*, pp. 211-12.
153 Ibid., pp. 212-13.
154 'Australian Political Chronicle July-December 1981', p. 102.
155 Ibid., p. 102.
156 Peel, 'Lindsay Thompson', pp. 319-20.
157 Thompson, *I Remember*, p. 213.
158 Colebatch, *Dick Hamer*, p. 410.
159 'Australian Political Chronicle July-December 1981', p. 102.
160 Foley, 'The Liberal Party Campaign', pp. 37-38.
161 Thompson, *I Remember*, p. 222.
162 Ibid., p. 223.
163 Thompson, *I Remember*, p. 223.
164 'Australian Political Chronicle July-December 1981', p. 102.
165 'Australian Political Chronicle January-June 1982', *AJPH*, Vol. 28, Issue 3, December 1982, pp. 443-44.
166 Ibid., pp. 443-44.
167 Thompson, *I Remember*, p. 225.
168 Ibid., p. 228; 'Australian Political Chronicle January-June 1982', p. 444.
169 Thompson, *I Remember*, p. 225.
170 'Australian Political Chronicle January-June 1982', p. 444.
171 Thompson, *I Remember*, p. 227.
172 Ibid., p. 227; Peel, 'Lindsay Thompson', p. 321.
173 'Australian Political Chronicle January-June 1982', p. 444.
174 Thompson, *I Remember*, p. 228.
175 Colebatch, *Dick Hamer*, pp. 409-10.
176 *Age*, 5 April 1982.
177 *Age*, 5 April 1982.
178 Thompson, *I Remember*, p. 235; VPD (LA), 4 November 1982, p. 1631.
179 *VPD* (LA), 29 July 2008, p. 2713.
180 *VPD* (LA), 4 November 1982, p. 1616.
181 Ibid., p. 1623.
182 Ibid., p. 1627.
183 Peel, 'Lindsay Thompson', p. 323.

184   *Age*, 18 July 2008.

185   *VPD* (LA), 4 November 1982, p. 1612.

186   *Age*, 29 May 1981.

187   *VPD*, 3 October 1962, p. 591.

188   *VPD*, 25 March 1975, p. 4483.

189   *VPD* (LA), 4 November 1982, pp. 1621.

190   *Canberra Times*, 3 June 1981.

191   *Age*, 27 June 1979.

192   *Age*, 29 March 1982.

193   *VPD* (LA), 4 November 1982, pp. 1630.

194   Walter Jona, *People, Parliament and Politics*, Tertiary Press, Melbourne, 2006, p. 93.